Mark Twain

HAYDN MIDDLETON

Heinemann Library
Chicago, Illinois

Customer Service 888-454-2279
Visit our website at www.heinemannlibrary.com

Designed by Tinstar Design
Originated by Ambassador Litho.
Printed and bound in Hong Kong/China

06 05 04 03 02
10 9 8 7 6 5 4 3 2 1

Library of Congress Cataloging-in-Publication Data
Middleton, Haydn.
  Mark Twain / Haydn Middleton.
     p. cm. -- (Creative lives)
Includes bibliographical references and index.
  ISBN 1-58810-205-X (lib. bdg.)
  1. Twain, Mark, 1835-1910--Juvenile literature. 2. Authors,
American--19th century--Biography--Juvenile literature. [1. Twain, Mark,
1835-1910. 2. Authors, American.] I. Title. II. Series.
  PS1331 .M48 2001
  818'.409--dc21

                              2001000530

Acknowledgments
The author and publishers are grateful to the following for permission to reproduce
copyright material: Mark Twain Memorial: pp. 4, 49; The Mark Twain Project/ The Bancroft
Library: pp. 5, 7, 9, 16, 21, 28, 36, 50; Mary Evans Picture Library: pp. 10, 11, 14, 15, 18, 33,
40, 44; Mark Twain House: pp. 12, 19, 23, 25, 26, 29, 32, 37, 42, 45, 46, 47, 51, 52; Peter
Newark's American Pictures: pp. 24, 35; The Kobal Collection: pp. 30, 39; Hulton Getty: p. 41;
Mark Twain Archive, Elmira College, New York: p. 54.
Cover photograph reproduced with permission of Corbis.

Some words are shown in bold, **like this.** You can find out what they mean by looking
in the glossary.

Contents

A Man Who
Filled Up the World

Mark Twain was born on February 3, 1863. This was the date that Samuel Langhorne Clemens first signed his writing with the name "Mark Twain," and invented an American author whose **novels** and stories are still popular today. Samuel Langhorne Clemens was born in Missouri in 1835. He died in 1910, when he was 74 years old. For nearly 50 of those 74 years he was known as Mark Twain, so that is the name we will use for him throughout this book. Mark Twain was the name he put on the covers of some of the best-loved books in American literature. It was also the name he used to give talks and tell stories to huge audiences all over the world.

Katy Leary, his servant for over 30 years, said that when he was away on his travels, "you always missed Mr. Clemens so. He was one of them people that just filled up the world for you." The famous writer Mark Twain filled up the world with pleasure. He wrote for adults and he wrote for children. He wrote best-selling travel books and he wrote adventure stories.

This is Sam Clemens around 1871 or 1875, when he was well on his way to achieving worldwide fame as the author Mark Twain.

> **"** "[Twain] invented a new style of writing, new **narrative** voices, and particularly American forms of humor and storytelling that were embraced by readers around the world long before the critics understood that he was not just popular, but was one of the originators of what they would call 'modern' literature." **"**
> Emory Elliott, professor of English at the University of California, Riverside

He wrote great comedy and he wrote with deadly seriousness. He did not write for highly educated people, but for ordinary folks just like him.

The first great international celebrity

"I have never tried… to help cultivate the cultivated classes," Twain once said. By *cultivated classes* Twain meant rich and well-educated people. "I was not equipped for it… and I never had any ambition in that direction." His goal, Twain said, was to write for "bigger game—the masses."

As a boy, Mark Twain was one of the masses himself. And even though he later became rich and famous, he never lost touch with his roots. In fact, he kept going back to these roots to look for creative inspiration. He grew up in the state of Missouri at

This photograph shows Mark Twain as an old man, in 1909. He once said that humor was "mankind's greatest blessing." Twain blessed millions of people by finding so much humor in life and recording it in his books.

5

a time when white people still owned black slaves, and he had black playmates as a child. He always remembered the way that African Americans spoke, joked, and told stories, and he reproduced it in some of his books. This was highly unusual, since there was still a great deal of **racism** in Twain's times. Some white readers believed Twain was wrong to show such interest in African-American culture. Other readers believed that his writing style was too conversational to be great literature. But Twain was ahead of his time. Today he is seen as a classic American author, and one who played a important part in defining an American national identity for the rest of the world.

Most of Twain's work is about American life, but he is popular all over the world. Anyone who loved a good story loved Twain's books. By the

Huckleberry Finn

Mark Twain's *Adventures of Huckleberry Finn* is thought by many to be the greatest American **novel,** but many people disapproved of the book when it was published. People were shocked that Twain would write about poor people like the main characters, Huck Finn and Jim. They also did not like that Twain wrote the book using **dialect** instead of using formal writing. The opening paragraph of the book is written as if Huck Finn were talking to the reader:

"You don't know about me, without you have read a book by the name of *The Adventures of Tom Sawyer* but that ain't no matter. That book was made by Mr. Mark Twain, and he told the truth, mainly. There was things which he stretched, but mainly he told the truth. That is nothing. I never seen anybody but lied, one time or another, without it was Aunt Polly, or the widow, or maybe Mary. Aunt Polly—Tom's Aunt Polly, she is— and Mary, and the Widow Douglas, is all told about in that book—which is mostly a true book; with some **stretchers,** as I said before."

end of his life he was an international celebrity. Many of the thousands who **mourned** Twain's death had never actually read his books. But they knew all about him, and about the ups and downs of his life.

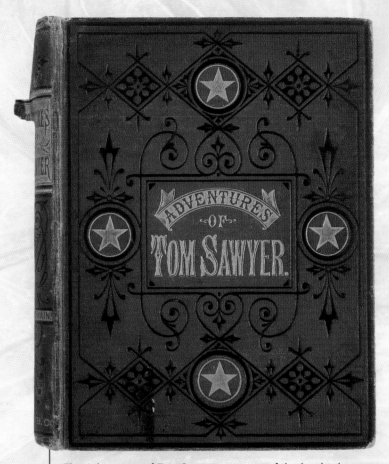

The Adventures of Tom Sawyer was one of the books that helped to make Mark Twain one of the most popular writers of the nineteenth century. Although it was about life in the U.S., readers all over the world enjoyed this story about children growing up in a small town.

" *It is my conviction that the human race is no proper target for harsh words and bitter criticisms, and that the only proper feeling toward it is compassion.*" In his *Autobiography of Mark Twain*, Mark Twain explained why he used humor, not angry words, to try to change society.

Life in the Midwest

In the early nineteenth century, the United States was expanding across the North American continent. In the West, new states were still being added by the government, which was buying the territory or defeating the Native American tribes who lived there. Missouri became a state in 1821. Growing up there was not easy. John Marshall Clemens and his wife, Jane, lost three of their seven children before the age of ten. The sixth, Samuel, was born on November 30, 1835. He was two months **premature,** and weighed just over 4⅓ pounds (2 kilograms). "A lady came in one day," his mother wrote later, "[and] said 'you don't expect to raise that babe, do you?' I said I would try. But he was a poor-looking object to raise." Samuel's birth coincided with an extraordinary sight in the night sky: the rare appearance of **Halley's Comet.** Later on, as Mark Twain, Samuel would compare himself to the comet, saying that, like the comet, he was an "unaccountable freak."

Making ends meet in Missouri

Mark Twain's father was known as Judge Clemens. He owned a store, and was a justice of the peace, but he did not make much money in either job. He lived in the hope of becoming rich through business **investments,** but he never managed to turn this hope into reality. Twain remembered him as "stern, unsmiling, never demonstrating affection for wife and child … ungentle of manner toward his children, but always a gentleman in his phrasing." Just before he died, in 1847, he kissed his daughter Pamela. It was the first and last time anyone in the family saw him show affection to his children.

Twain went to school from the age of five to age thirteen, but he did not do well. He always needed more love than he got. Maybe that was why, from a young age, he playfully sought attention and approval from those around him. He had a slow, **drawling** voice, and discovered he could entertain people by telling them stories. In addition to being able to tell stories, Twain had realistic dreams, and thought he could see into the future. He dreamed about the death of

*"Brick commercial buildings lined Market Street and large warehouses rose by the river ... houses of stone and brick and fancy clapboard went up where rustic pioneer cabins had once stood as people made fortunes in the **burgeoning** trade passing through Hannibal ... Hannibal also began making steamboat hulls, to be floated downriver and outfitted in St. Louis. At one of the first boat launchings, when Sam was nine, people gathered by the shore to cheer as the hull splashed into Bear Creek. No sooner had the **hoopla** begun than Sam appeared on deck, waving his hat to the excited crowd."*

This passage from *Inventing Mark Twain*, by Andrew Hoffman, shows how Twain's hometown was growing as he was growing up.

This photograph shows Mark Twain at age fifteen, a few years after he left school for good. He was working as a typesetter at a newspaper at this time, and he is holding a row of type that spells out his real name.

his sister Margaret just before it happened. Later, in 1858, he dreamed that his brother Henry was dead. Soon after the dream, Henry died in a river accident. Twain became afraid that he had supernatural powers.

From 1835 the Clemens family lived in the growing town of Hannibal, Missouri, on the banks of the Mississippi River. Years later, when Sam Clemens became Mark Twain, he would write a lot about this town in **antebellum** times, calling it by the fictional name of St. Petersburg.

Mark Twain grew up by the banks of the Mississippi River, called "The Big Muddy," and dreamed of one day becoming a steamboat pilot.

Printing and piloting

Just before his father's death, Twain began an **apprenticeship** as a printer with the *Missouri Courier*, a local newspaper. Later he worked for a time as a **journeyman** and reporter for the *Hannibal Journal*. His older brother Orion was in the printing and publishing business, but never made much money. Twain assisted Orion for a while, then left home to travel and work on **typesetting** in places ranging from St. Louis to New York. Before leaving Hannibal, his mother made him promise to stay away from card games and alcohol, which is a clue about what his interests were at that time.

> " *"I was born lazy. I am no lazier now than I was 40 years ago, but that is because I reached the limit 40 years ago. You can't go beyond possibility."* Twain claimed that he was lazy when he described his early jobs." "

Twain learned a lot about writing in his job as a printer. "One isn't a printer ten years," he said in 1909, "without setting up acres of good and bad literature, and learning—unconsciously at first, consciously later—to discriminate between the two ... and meanwhile ... consciously acquiring what is called a style." Twain also made up for his poor education. In a letter to his brother he mentions spending a lot of time in two New York printers' libraries.

Occasionally Twain wrote short pieces for his brother's local newspapers. A **sketch** titled "The Dandy Frightening the Squatter" was published in the Boston *Carpet Bag* in 1852. But Mark Twain, although he was tired of printing, was not yet ready to make writing his full-time job. "When I was a boy," he later wrote in *Life on the Mississippi*, "there was but one permanent ambition among my comrades. That was, to be a steamboatman." For four years, from 1857 to 1861, Twain got to work in the job he had wanted ever since he was a boy.

The Mississippi steamboat was essential to trade in the years before the American Civil War (1861–65). Twain learned to read the water between St. Louis and New Orleans so well that he could steer at night "the way you follow a hall at home in the dark—because you know the shape of it."

Twain would later write that a steamboat pilot was the only *"entirely independent human being that lived in the earth ... I have seen a boy of eighteen taking a great steamer serenely into what seemed almost certain destruction, and the aged captain standing mutely by, filled with apprehension but powerless to interfere."*

Twain completed his **apprenticeship** to become a steamboat pilot on the Mississippi River, and got his license on April 9, 1859. His trainer was a pilot who liked to quote passages from Shakespeare while he was at the wheel, mixed in with curses and commands. "I have never since been able to read Shakespeare in a calm and sane way," Twain recalled in 1909. He also claimed to have "loved the profession far better than any I have followed since."

But despite his love of the river, and his love of the people he worked with, Twain would not work as a pilot for long. In 1861 the American Civil War began, and the steamboats stopped running.

This photo of Twain was taken while he was working on the river. He liked to wear his hair long. Later, his long, white hair and white suits would identify him as Mark Twain, the famous author.

Two weeks as a soldier

The Civil War between North and South divided not only the American nation, but also divided states like Missouri, and sometimes families within those states. In the case of uncertain men like Twain, it could even leave individuals feeling divided. "There was a good deal of confusion in men's minds during the first months of the trouble," he wrote in 1885, "a good deal of unsettledness, of leaning first this way, then that, then the other way."

Twain's first response to the war was to show loyalty to the South. He volunteered to join the Marion Rangers, a **Confederate militia** based near the town of Florida, Missouri. He lasted for just two weeks as a soldier, "hunted like a rat the whole time" by **Union** troops under Ulysses S. Grant, the commander of the Union army. Twain would later say that during his two weeks as a soldier he learned more about retreating "than the man that invented retreating." He dropped out of the Marion Rangers and made up with his brother Orion, who had remained loyal to the Union. Orion had been appointed Secretary of the Nevada Territory, and in July 1861, the brothers left Missouri for new adventures in the West.

The American Civil War, 1861–65

This bitter war was fought between the Northern, or Union, states and the Southern, or Confederate, states. People in the South were determined to maintain slavery, even though the rest of the U.S. wanted to make it illegal. They separated from the rest of the U.S., because they thought that the individual states should be able to decide whether or not slavery would be legal. People in the North fought to keep the U.S. together. In 1863, President Abraham Lincoln issued the **Emancipation** Proclamation, freeing all American slaves, but the war went on for two more years. Lincoln was assassinated before the proclamation could take effect in the South.

On the Jumping Frog to Fame

Many people headed West in the 1860s. They dreamed of making their fortunes in the new territories of Nevada and California. In 1861, Mark Twain arrived in Nevada in the company of his brother, Orion, with a job as a government clerk. Five years later he left alone, disappointed in all his business ventures, but with a fine and growing reputation in two new professions. The first was as a humorous journalist; the second was as a humorous public lecturer. He also left the West under the **pseudonym** he used when he wrote and lectured so successfully, and which he was now using full time.

Mark Twain is born

On February 3, 1863, Sam Clemens signed a humorous travel letter to the *Territorial Enterprise*, a newspaper in Virginia City, Nevada, "Yours, dreamily, Mark Twain." Why did he choose that name? The author later said he borrowed it from an old Mississippi steamboat pilot. There is also a story that he took it from the Nevada saloonkeepers' habit of marking down only two, or twain, drinks on credit before the drinker had to pay. Most people now believe the name is copied from the steamboat pilot's cry when the river was measured at two fathoms (twelve feet) deep. This meant the boat could travel

To travel to Nevada, Sam and Orion had to take a 20-day stagecoach journey from St. Joseph, Missouri. St. Joseph was also the starting point of the famous **Pony Express.**

through it safely. Some critics think Mark Twain also chose the name to alert his readers to the fact that his writing had at least two levels of meaning: both funny and serious.

Going back to print

The wide open spaces of Nevada and California were rough-and-ready places in the 1860s. Towns like Carson City and Virginia City were full of hard-headed, hard-drinking miners and **prospectors.** There were very few women around. Twain tried his luck in a silver mine, buying into it because he was sure he would get rich on silver. He lost money on the mine, and lost more money on poker games.

He continued to run up debts even after he got a writing job with the *Territorial Enterprise* newspaper in Virginia City. The town, just five years old, was full of dangerous men. According to local legend, the first 26 graves in its cemetery were occupied by murdered men. Twain did his best to cut a controversial figure around town. With his old clothes and drawling speech, some people thought he was a drunken idiot. But his witty articles won him fans at once. He wrote local news, personal **satire,** travel pieces, and sometimes downright hoaxes. For example, in one article he made up a story about the mysterious movements of several boulders in the Nevada desert. He described the boulders in great detail to make people think his story was true.

Artemus Ward, "the prince of platform entertainers," was one of Twain's friends in the West. His humorous lectures helped inspire Twain to speak in public.

Within a year Twain wrote to his mother, "I am prone to boast of having the widest reputation, as a local editor, of any man on the Pacific Coast."

Twain's big break came when he heard a funny **saloon** story in the Mother Lode hills of California. He summarized it like this in his notebook: "Coleman with his jumping frog—bet a stranger $50.— Stranger had no frog and C. got him one:—In the meantime stranger filled C's frog full of **shot** and he couldn't jump. The stranger's frog won." He wrote it up as "Jim Smiley and His Jumping Frog," and on the advice of his friend, Artemus Ward, sent it east to the New York *Saturday Press*, which happily published it.

But that was just the start. As more and more newspapers got hold of the story, the "Jumping Frog" became famous across the country. The name of its author, Mark Twain, won plenty of attention too. Twain was also pleased with the story. He wrote "It is the best humorous **sketch** America has produced yet, and I must read it in public some day." Already his thoughts were moving beyond the page to the stage. In 1866, he got his chance to start performing.

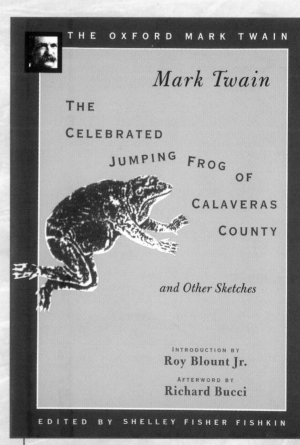

THE OXFORD MARK TWAIN

Mark Twain

THE CELEBRATED JUMPING FROG OF CALAVERAS COUNTY

and Other Sketches

INTRODUCTION BY
Roy Blount Jr.

AFTERWORD BY
Richard Bucci

EDITED BY SHELLEY FISHER FISHKIN

Twain later renamed his story *The Celebrated Jumping Frog of Calaveras County*. It is still in print, and is still enjoyed by people around the world.

Mark Twain on the stage

For five months in 1866, Twain left the American mainland. The Sacramento *Union* paper sent him to Oahu, Maui, and Hawaii, the Sandwich Islands, which are now part of the state of Hawaii. His job was to describe what he found. He scored a **scoop** in June by reporting on the burning of the clipper ship *Hornet*. His article about the survivors, "Forty-three Days in an Open Boat," was also published in *Harper's New Monthly Magazine*, which brought him more popularity, this time as a serious writer.

But Twain found plenty that was funny, too. On his return to San Francisco he decided that he was ready to take to the public stage. He rented a theater, Maguire's Academy of Music, and then published promotional **handbills** that said: "A splendid orchestra is in town, but has not been engaged ... Magnificent fireworks were in contemplation for the occasion, but the idea has been abandoned ..." The public was not too confused by these to attend the event on the evening of October 2, 1866. Many in the packed audience were Twain's personal friends. Others were **creditors** who came expecting to be paid. After a moment's stage fright, Twain proved to be a mesmerizing public speaker. He kept the audience's attention as he told them of the wonders of the Sandwich Islands. He made them roar with laughter as he described how the Kanaka people would "feed their dogs, pet them, take ever so much care of them, and then cook and eat them."

His show was such a success that he took it to Sacramento, and on to other California towns. In San Jose he offered to demonstrate Hawaiian cannibalism if a young mother in the audience would give him her child to eat. Mark Twain had discovered the excitement of the stage. For the rest of his life, he would never be able to give it up.

> "
> *"Nothing so needs reforming as other people's habits."*
> *"Few things are harder to put up with than the annoyance of a good example."*
> "
> These are examples of the kinds of witty remarks Mark Twain would make on stage.

An Innocent Abroad

" The editor of *Round Table* in New York said, "*The foremost among the merry gentlemen of the California press, as far as we have been able to judge, is the one who signs himself Mark Twain.*"

"*Make your mark on New York, and you are a made man. With a New York endorsement you may travel the country over without fear,*" Mark Twain wrote about his decision to move to the city. "

By moving West, Twain had been able to avoid the Civil War in the East. But the war ended in 1865, and Twain became more and more interested in doing speaking tours on the East Coast, too. "Jim Smiley and His Jumping Frog" had made Twain popular on the East Coast, and people there were interested in seeing him on stage.

In 1867, New York looked like this. "It keeps a stranger in a state of unwholesome excitement all the time," according to Twain.

Twain on tour

In 1867, as traveling correspondent for the *Alta California*, Twain moved to New York. He sent back a stream of reports on the city, its sights, and its celebrities. He also toured theaters on the East Coast and in the Midwest. Posters announced him as "the greatest humorist in America," and audiences everywhere seemed to agree. Already he was more popular than famous humorists like Artemus Ward, Petroleum V. Nasby, and Josh Billings. The publication of his first book, *The Celebrated Jumping Frog of Calaveras County and Other Sketches,* helped his popularity too, even though it was not an immediate best-seller.

Twain (standing) is shown here with two other popular humorists, Petroleum V. Nasby, and Josh Billings, in 1869.

> "Mark Twain is a very good-looking man. He is of medium height and moderately slender build, has light brown hair, a reddish brown moustache, regular features and a fresh complexion; and he has a queer way of wrinkling up his nose and half closing his eyes when he speaks ... Looking at him you feel it to be an impossibility that he should ever hurry or be out of temper, and you might suppose him to be incapable of a joke, if it were not for the peculiar twinkle in his merry eyes ... His style of speaking is unique to the last degree ... He delivers his sentences without haste, and in a tone of utter indifference."

This review of Twain's lectures was printed in the *Boston Advertiser*, in 1869.

Later that year Twain got a chance to travel even farther away. He left New York for a five-month tour of Europe and the Middle East on a ship called *The Quaker City*. This adventure was good for his reputation as a writer and as a **humorist.** Readers back home waited eagerly for his reports from abroad. When he returned, he lectured to large crowds of fans, and wrote a book about the whole trip, which he called *The Innocents Abroad*. It was published in 1869, and within two years it had sold 100,000 copies. This was a large sales figure for the time, and it was an especially large number of sales for a humorous book.

Before Mark Twain, most American writing about Europe was **reverent.** Most Americans wrote about the great art and beautiful buildings they saw in European cities. They wrote about the brilliant philosophers and writers who lived in the cities, and about the old universities that they saw. Most Americans respected the European capitals, and felt that their young country could not compete with the art, history, learning, and traditions of Europe. Twain wanted to change that. He said he wanted "to suggest to the reader how he [the reader] would be likely to see Europe and the East if he looked at them with his own eyes instead of the eyes of those who traveled in those countries before him." So he made remarks like, "They spell it *Vinci* and pronounce it *Vinchy*; foreigners always spell better than they pronounce." And he called the Holy Land a shabby landscape of rocks and camel dung. As for Moses leading the children of Israel from Egypt to the Promised Land, Twain joked that it took Moses 40 years, "while the overland stage could have done it in 36 hours."

By laughing along with Twain's account of his travels, Americans could feel less like the uncultured relations of the grand old Europeans. The United States was a young country. It was still developing an American style of art, education, and national traditions, but it was already becoming a major **economic** power. Twain's message to his readers was clear: if the U.S. was going to lead the way into the future, its citizens needed to start by changing the way they felt about the past.

Livy: the love of his life

Around Christmas, 1867, Twain had his first date with Olivia Langdon, the sister of a man he had traveled with on *The Quaker City*. Olivia, called Livy, was 22 when they met, and Twain was 32. Twain took her to hear Charles Dickens give a public reading. Twain later recalled that Dickens earned $200,000 from his readings in the U.S. that season, but his date with Livy "made the fortune of my life—not in dollars ... it made the real fortune of my life in that it made the happiness of my life." On February 2, 1870, Twain and Livy were married, after overcoming her parents' objections.

The Langdon family was not impressed by Twain's poor family, drinking, smoking, and lack of religious beliefs. They made him promise to reform. In over 200 letters to Livy, Twain swore that he would change for her sake. But a few years into the marriage he was drinking and smoking again.

This image shows Olivia "Livy" Langdon as she looked around the time she met Twain. For years she acted as his closest adviser, and read all of his manuscripts and gave her suggestions.

" *"Grief can take care of itself; but to get the full value of a joy you must have somebody to divide it with."* Twain, from *Following the Equator*

Success at Last

At the start of the 1870s, life seemed good to Mark Twain. By the age of 35 the poor boy from Hannibal, Missouri, was famous on both sides of the Atlantic Ocean. He also had a beautiful wife from a highly respected East Coast family, and was living in a mansion in Buffalo, New York. This was a wedding gift from his father-in-law, who had also helped Twain to become part owner of the Buffalo *Express*, a local newspaper. He enjoyed his work on the newspaper, and he and Livy were expecting their first child.

Building a family and a home

Livy's pregnancy, however, was very difficult. Livy had suffered from bad health ever since she was a child, and the pregnancy made her weak and tired. When her father died in August 1870, she had an emotional breakdown and became very sick. The baby was born **prematurely** in November, and was a weak and sickly boy who she and Twain named Langdon. He lived for a year and ten months, but he died in September 1872.

By that time Livy had given birth to a second child, a daughter named Susy. The death of her son led to another breakdown. Twain was also depressed. He felt grief and also felt guilty—just as he had when his own brothers and sister had died. He wondered if the death of his son was punishment for the fame and the money he was earning through his books. Soon it was clear that this was not true, as the little family began to grow. A second daughter, Clara, was born in 1874, and was followed by another daughter, Jean, who was born in 1880.

Twain worked harder than before at his writing and lecturing in order to support his growing family, and he became more and more successful. In 1871 he had sold his share in the Buffalo *Express* and also sold the home that had been given to him. He wanted to go on being a high achiever, but only on his own terms. This involved moving to Nook Farm, a suburb of Hartford, Connecticut. Nook Farm was a wealthy community, and it already was home to many famous writers, including Harriet Beecher Stowe and Charles Dudley Warner. But none

This photograph is of the Twains' house in Nook Farm. "Mr. Clemens seems to glory in his sense of possession," Livy wrote in 1874, just after the family moved in.

of them owned a home like the mansion that Twain built for his family, and moved into in 1874. It was the landmark in the neighborhood, because it was so large and strange looking. One of Twain's biographers, Justin Kaplan, described it as "part steamboat, part medieval stronghold, part cuckoo clock."

Working practices

Twain's new home had nineteen rooms, including a guest room shaped like a steamboat's pilothouse and a schoolroom, where the children were taught by Livy and a governess. It cost Twain $125,000 to build the house, an enormous amount at the time. He would spend a lot more money on the furniture to fill the house and on the many alterations he made to the house in the next few years.

Ironically, he could never work in his big, new, second-floor study. He always concentrated better at the family's small summer house at

23

Quarry Farm, near Elmira, New York. He liked to have peace and quiet to write, and on most days he worked from breakfast until late afternoon without a break. He loved, he wrote to a friend in 1883, "to step straight into the study, damp from the breakfast table, and sail right in and sail right on, the whole day long, without thought of running short of stuff or words. I wrote 4,000 words today and I touch 3,000 and upwards pretty often, and don't fall below 2,600 on any working day."

Mark Twain at home

Twain never forgot what it was like to grow up poor. He was determined that his own children would grow up surrounded by love and money. At their Hartford home he tried to create a safe, enjoyable world for them and for Livy—a decent place in an age that he found more and more indecent. Although Twain wanted to be rich to make his family secure, he hated the greed and **corruption** he observed in politicians and businessmen. He regularly attacked the "rottenness" of his time in writings like *The Gilded Age*.

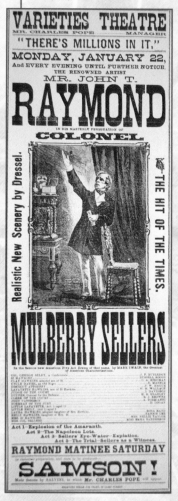

In 1873 Twain published a novel, *The Gilded Age*, which he co-wrote very quickly with Charles Dudley Warner. Twain later turned the book into a successful play. This handbill advertises the play.

He filled up his home with servants, including two maids, a laundry woman, a cook, and a coachman, and he entertained a constant stream of neighbors, visitors, and celebrities. He relied on his butler, George Griffin, to control the huge number of fans, well-wishers, and beggars who also visited. George came to wash the windows one day and never left. He was a bad butler, but he laughed at Twain's jokes and the two men became good friends. When visitors came, George would take their calling cards to Twain in the **billiard** room. Twain would shout and swear that he did not want to see them, and then George would translate his words into a kind refusal.

His house and entertaining were expensive, so Twain had to keep money coming in. He did this by turning himself into, in his own words, "the busiest ... man in America." He lectured, wrote newspaper articles, and wrote a book about his days in Nevada and California, called *Roughing It*. The book sold well, and brought Twain a lot of money.

This photograph shows Twain's conservatory. It was expensive to keep up, but he wanted Livy to have flowers during the long winters.

Roughing It

Twain was proud of the way his descriptive writing improved in *Roughing It*, and pleased that the book was praised by reviewers. Here he describes watching a **Pony Express** rider approaching his coach:

"In a second or two it becomes horse and rider, rising and falling, rising and falling—sweeping toward us nearer and nearer— growing more and more distinct, more and more sharply defined— nearer and still nearer, and the flutter of the hooves comes faintly to the ear—another instant a whoop and a hurrah from our upper deck, a wave of the rider's hand, but no reply, and man and horse burst past our excited faces, and winging away like the belated fragment of a storm."

But Twain still had an eye for money-making ideas besides writing. He was never one to take heed of his own advice: "There are two times in a man's life when he should not **speculate:** when he can't afford it, and when he can." He got involved in trying to make money on all sorts of strange ideas: a board game featuring pegs and pins, a **still** for desalting water, an improved steam engine for tugboats, and, last but not least, "Mark Twain's Self-Pasting Scrapbook." This was a book with strips of glue on the pages. You rubbed the glue with a damp sponge, and then put a picture or piece of paper on it. Twain liked to keep newspaper clippings, and designed this invention for his own use. It was the only investment that did make him extra money: during his lifetime, he sold more copies of this book than any of his **novels.**

This photo shows Twain wearing his sealskin winter outfit. He always liked to wear strange clothes that would make people turn and look at him.

Tired books

These other interests kept Twain busy as he was struggling to write a new novel. As he said in his *Autobiography of Mark Twain:* "It was by accident that I found out a book is pretty sure to get tired about the middle and refuse to go on with its work until its powers and its interests should have been refreshed by a rest ... It was when I had reached the middle of *Tom Sawyer* that I made this invaluable find. At page 400 of my manuscript the story made a sudden and determined halt, and refused to proceed another step."

Twain had been doing very well with the book, writing about 50 pages a day, until he got stuck. He was frustrated with writing, and thought he would never finish the novel. He put his manuscript away for two years, and worked on lectures, newspaper articles, and overseeing his **investments** instead. After a two-year break, he was back to his 50-page-a-day pace, and was soon able to finish what would become one of his most famous books.

"It is written for adults"

In 1876, Twain published *The Adventures of Tom Sawyer.* Strangely, even though Twain's popularity was growing in the U.S. and Europe, the book was not a best-seller at once. It had some glowing reviews, but sold only about 24,000 copies in its first year. Twain set the book in the simpler, more innocent **antebellum** era. His model for the town where the book takes place was his hometown of Hannibal, Missouri, which he renamed St. Petersburg, and his childhood friends served as models for the main characters. Readers enjoyed the adventures of the book's young heroes—Tom Sawyer and Huckleberry Finn—because they were always getting into funny messes. The book helped people remember what life was like in the days before the Civil War. At the same time, Twain's text presented readers with many sharp criticisms of the way that American life was changing.

Twain always intended the book to be for adult readers. Originally, he wanted to write about Tom's entire life, including trips to foreign places and then a final return to St. Petersburg. But he became so interested in writing about Tom as a boy that he never got him through to adulthood. As a result, the book was **marketed** for young readers. Twain disliked his publisher's decision to sell the **novel** as a book for children. He told his publisher, "It is not a boy's book, at all. It will only be read by adults. It is only written for adults." Twain had never written anything like *Tom Sawyer* before, and he was not sure that the novel was good. In later years *Tom Sawyer* became a much-loved classic, and it still sells more copies than any other book by Twain. But after it was first published, Twain felt very uncertain about his future writing novels. "If I can make a living out of plays," he wrote in a letter, "I shall never write another book. For the present I have placed the three books in my mind in the wastebasket."

This illustration by True Williams was in the first edition of *The Adventures of Tom Sawyer*. Williams, an alcoholic, illustrated many of Twain's books. Twain worried about Williams's drinking, and wrote about him, "What a genius he has, and how he does murder it with rum."

Despite what he said, Twain was soon working on novels again. He began writing *The Prince and the Pauper*, and some chapters of a new novel set in America. Then, in 1878, he took his family to Europe to research and write another travel book, *A Tramp Abroad*. They visited Germany, Switzerland, Italy, France, and England, and returned to Nook Farm in 1879. Twain came home refreshed by the long break. Livy soon gave birth to their third daughter, Jean. There could be little doubt that the 1870s had been Twain's best decade yet.

This photo is of Livy with (left to right) Susy, Clara, and Jean in 1884. Twain loved his family, and insisted that they go with him on his trips and lecture tours.

Time for Twain's Best Book

Just after Twain returned from Europe, an old friend, Mary Fairbanks, wrote to him: "The time has come for your *best book*. I do not mean your book with the most money in it, I mean your best contribution to American literature." Maybe Twain agreed with her. Maybe he even realized that he had already started his best book. Soon after finishing *Tom Sawyer* he started to work on a **sequel:** the autobiography of the **novel's** other main character, Huckleberry Finn. Huck was an ignorant village boy—a social outcast, a liar, and a thief, with no respect for authority. Twain chose to let him tell his own story. This was a brave decision. Educated Americans thought people like Huck were ignorant and unimportant. A book telling his story might not sell well, and could damage Twain's reputation.

Errol Flynn starred in the 1937 movie of Twain's *The Prince and the Pauper*. In this story, set in Tudor England, Prince Edward and a poor man named Tom Canty find out about each other's way of life.

For sixteen chapters, Twain believed the book was going well. Then, in the summer of 1876, he ran out of steam. This had happened to him as he wrote *The Adventures of Tom Sawyer* in 1874. He put the manuscript away to work on other projects, exactly what he had done to finish *Tom Sawyer*. One of the projects he worked on at this time was a game for teaching history.

> " Twain used the tale of *The Prince and the Pauper* to show Americans that fairy-tale accounts of Tudor England covered up social problems that still existed in the nineteenth century. *"There has never been a time,"* he pointed out, *"when above FOURTEEN crimes were punishable by death in Connecticut. But in England, within the memory of men who are still **hale** in body and mind, TWO HUNDRED AND TWENTY-THREE crimes were punishable by death!"* "

A productive period

In the early 1880s Twain was writing as fast and as much as ever. He had to, in order to pay his bills. By 1880, he was struggling to keep up the Nook Farm house, in spite of a large amount of money that he earned from his **royalties** and **investments.** In 1881 alone he spent about $100,000 on the house and entertaining the people who visited him there.

A Tramp Abroad was published in 1880. It was just a collection of short travel pieces, but it sold extremely well, because of Twain's humorous descriptions of travel. Three years later he published another successful nonfiction book, *Life on the Mississippi*. This book described the Mississippi River and the lives of the people who lived near it and worked on it. By now Twain was interested in the business side of publishing too. Twain would eventually become a publisher in his own right, risking a lot of money in his attempts to make even bigger profits by publishing books as well as writing them.

A third book that Twain worked on during this period was *The Prince and the Pauper*. Twain had not written historical fiction before, and he did it well. Like the Huckleberry Finn project that he had put away, this book mixed a good story with social criticism. But unlike the other project, this "good-mannered and agreeable" romance would not offend any of his readers. Reviews called it "pure," "lovely," "delicate," and "refined." The book would later become a children's classic, but in the early 1880s its sales did not match the sales of Twain's nonfiction.

On the road again

Another way of raising money was **speculating,** an activity that would lead Twain into a lot of trouble. He had less luck with business than with writing. One of his worst business decisions was to appoint his nephew, Charley Webster, as his business manager. By the time Webster died in 1891, he had cost Twain over $100,000. In addition to worrying about his nephew's bad business decisions, Twain had to worry about the **economy.** In 1884 there was a financial crisis, and because of his "losses, ill luck, and botched business," he began to have trouble keeping up with his bills.

To make more money, Twain went on a tour of 104 performances in four months, from November 1884, until the end of February 1885. This time, he organized the tour in addition to being a performer, and he invited his fellow novelist George Washington Cable to share the stage with him for readings, stories, and songs. They called themselves "Twins of Genius." Twain earned $17,000 from the tour. He used the tour as an opportunity to read and act out some chapters from his Huckleberry Finn project.

This photo shows Twain with George Washington Cable in 1884. The two men had the same sense of humor, and their tour was popular all over the country.

Ulysses S. Grant

Grant became famous as the commander of the **Union** army during the American Civil War. He became a member of the **Republican Party,** and was elected president in 1869, and again in 1872. Grant was an honest man, but he gave government jobs to some people who were **corrupt.** People began to distrust the government, and Grant did not run for president in 1877. He retired, and invested all of his money in a company that went bankrupt in 1884. To make money he wrote his *Memoirs,* but he died soon after the book was finished.

Meanwhile, Twain began work on a project with another person who lost money in the 1884 crisis, former U.S. President Ulysses S. Grant. Grant was one of many world leaders Twain had met. When he heard that Grant was planning to write his life story because he needed money, Twain insisted on publishing it. Charley Webster was involved in the project, but even he could not ruin the book. In late 1885, Twain published the *Personal Memoirs of U.S. Grant* with astonishing results. Over 200,000 copies of the book were sold. The book made almost $500,000 for Grant's family, and Twain's New York publishing company earned more than $200,000 on the book.

Ulysses S. Grant became president in 1869. He was a good general, but he was not a good president. He gave government jobs to his friends and family, and was not able to meet his political goals because of scandals.

33

"The best book we've had"

On February 18, 1885, almost a decade after Mark Twain started to write it, *Adventures of Huckleberry Finn* was published in the U.S. The book was very important to Twain. He could not rest until he got the story out on paper. In "Chapter the Last," you can hear the author's own relief at having finally succeeded. He has Huck say: "So there ain't nothing more to write about, and I am rotten glad of it, because if I'd a knowed what a trouble it was to make a book I wouldn't a tackled it and ain't agoing to no more."

The story is about Huck, a poor white boy running away from his cruel father, and Jim, an intelligent African-American man, trying to escape and free his family from slavery. The two of them manage to overcome their differences and become loyal friends. They are determined to escape the ignorant, **racist,** and cruel people in their community, and they give each other hope and courage. Twain described it as "a book of mine where a sound heart and a deformed conscience come into collision and conscience suffers defeat." By "sound heart" he meant Huck and Jim's courage and loyalty, and by "deformed conscience" he meant the customs and traditions of the people who try to hurt Huck and Jim.

On one level, *Huckleberry Finn* was a thrilling story about escape and freedom. On another, it was an **allegory** of the lost innocence of the U.S. The story was set in **antebellum** times, but Twain was describing what was wrong with the U.S. in the 1870s and 1880s, in business, in politics, in race relations, and in moral values. In 1885 plenty of American readers were not ready for this. In March, the Library Committee of Concord, Massachusetts, removed the book from the library shelves, saying it was "rough, coarse, and inelegant ... more suited to the slums than to intelligent, respectable people." Twain knew that even the criticism of the book was good publicity. He wrote: "They have expelled Huck from their library as 'trash and suitable only for the slums.' That will sell 25,000 copies for us for sure."

People are still arguing about the book's language and plot.

There was a mixed response to *Adventures of Huckleberry Finn* when it first appeared. People still disagree about the book today.

Adventures of Huckleberry Finn has sold millions of copies, and has been translated into many different languages, but it is banned from many school reading lists and libraries. The book is so famous that even people who have never read it have strong opinions about whether or not it should be available in libraries, or assigned to be read in school.

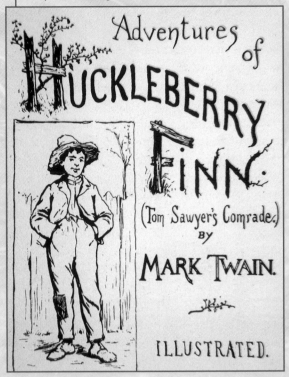

Adventures of
HUCKLEBERRY
FINN.
(Tom Sawyer's Comrade.)
BY
MARK TWAIN.

ILLUSTRATED.

" *Adventures of Huckleberry Finn* has always been controversial. Here are "
some opinions from people who have liked or disliked the book:

"If Mr. Clemens cannot think of something better to tell our pure-minded lads and lasses, he had better stop writing for them."
– Author Louisa M. Alcott, 1885

"It's the best book we've had. All American writing comes from that. There was nothing before."
– Author Ernest Hemingway, 1938

*"The **prejudicial** effect of the racial characterizations outweighs any literary value that the book might have."*
– Cherry Hill Minority Civic Association, 1996

"Can you end racism in the United States by shielding students from language and issues that make them uncomfortable, or does it need to be directly confronted, with Mark Twain's Huckleberry Finn *being one of the books that is most widely available for that purpose?"*
– Author Jim Zwick, 1997

Twain in Trouble

Twain turned 50 at the end of 1885, and was honored by people all over the world. He was full of contradictions—he was both funny and serious, missed the past and was optimistic about the future, was both romantic and realistic—but these contradictions just seemed to make him more popular.

In spite of all of the praise that he received on his birthday, Twain was not sure that his books were good. In his notebook he wondered if his books were good or just popular: "My books are like water; those of the great geniuses are wine. Everybody drinks water." He continue to write popular and classic books. And, in the next ten years, he would depend on his popularity to help him through some difficult times.

In this picture, taken when he was around 50 years old, Twain presents himself as a successful businessman, wearing a top hat, suit, and tie.

"Poetry in steel"

The house in Nook Farm and Twain's visitors were costing him more than ever, but Twain's income and popularity seemed secure. However, he still longed to be a business hero, too. Maybe he was confused by his two identities. "Mark Twain" had fame, wealth, and honor. But what of "Sam Clemens," his true self? How could he become famous? He certainly spent time

This is the typesetting machine that was designed by James W. Paige. Mark Twain described it as "inspired," and "magnificent," but he lost a lot of money when a more efficient machine was invented before Paige finished this one.

thinking about this. He even started signing his name "S.L. Clemens," and writing "Mark Twain" over it at an angle. The autograph ended up looking like a dark cross, and the names seemed to cancel each other out.

In 1880, Twain had invested $5,000 in an automatic **typesetting** machine. The machine's inventor, James W. Paige, was building it at a factory in Hartford. Twain could hardly believe what he was seeing. He remembered how many workers and how much money it took to set type by hand. Now a single operator at a keyboard would be able to do the work much faster. Paige told Twain that his machine, or "mechanical marvel," as Twain called it, just needed a little more money. But every time Twain paid Paige to finish the machine, Paige asked him for more money. By February, 1886, Twain was still spending money on the project, and was using his publishing company as a private bank to pay for it. Meanwhile, another inventor was working on a machine that would remove the need for direct typesetting altogether.

Twain now decided to go for broke: he set up a company to complete, manufacture, and **market** the typesetter around the world. He believed that this piece of "poetry in steel" would make him a millionaire many times over. But by 1894 the machine had cost him $200,000, driving him into **bankruptcy.** Paige's machine had about 18,000 separate parts, and was almost impossible to assemble. For almost fifteen years it had taken up a huge amount of Twain's time, and it was never finished. Luckily, Twain had continued to write and lecture, and was able to make money on his books and lecture tours.

A so-called comic fantasy

From 1886 until 1889, Twain worked on one of his strangest books. George Washington Cable had introduced Twain to the British myth of King Arthur, and soon he started seeing comic possibilities in it.

A Connecticut Yankee in King Arthur's Court tells the story of Hank Morgan, a mechanic at the factory in Hartford where Paige's machine was being built. After being hit in the head, he wakes up near the mythical castle of Camelot, in England, in the sixth century. Morgan decides to bring "the great and **beneficent** civilization of the nineteenth century" to sixth-century England. At first the results are humorous, but the plot grows darker as it develops. Morgan does not understand what will happen when he introduces factories and schools

> **"** **"**
>
> *"Dream of being a knight errant in armor in the middle ages. Have the notions and habits of thought of the present day mixed with the necessities of that. No pockets in the armor. No way to manage certain requirements of nature. Can't scratch. Cold in the head—can't blow—can't get at handkerchief, can't use iron sleeve. Iron gets red hot in the sun—leaks in the rain, gets white with frost and freezes me solid in winter. Suffer from lice and fleas. Make disagreeable clatter when I enter church. Can't dress or undress myself. Always getting struck by lightning. Fall down, can't get up."*
>
> These are the first notes Twain made for *Connecticut Yankee.*

to sixth-century people. The machines that Morgan builds are a mixed blessing, and this might have been a reflection of Twain's feelings about Paige's machine. The book ends in a battle between Morgan and his supporters, and Morgan's enemies. According to Henry Nash Smith, the battle scene was "one of the most distressing passages in American literature." This was surprising, since Twain's book was sold as a "comic fantasy." The book got good reviews, but it did not sell as well as Twain had hoped it would.

Bing Crosby starred in a movie that made a musical out of Twain's *A Connecticut Yankee in King Arthur's Court*.

Back to Europe

Twain followed *A Connecticut Yankee in King Arthur's Court* with a **farce** called *The American Claimant*. This book did not sell well, and critics today say it is one of Twain's worst pieces of writing. Twain's health was not good at this time. As well as suffering from stress over money, his right hand was almost crippled with **rheumatism.** Twain solved this problem by learning to write left-handed, but as the 1880s turned into the 1890s, he struggled to find a new subject that interested him. He never finished *The Innocents Adrift*, a new travel book. Finally, he began another dark novel, *The Tragedy of Pudd'nhead Wilson*, which was published in 1894.

By this time, Twain was living in Europe, and staying in hotels for months at a time. In 1891 he and his family had left for Europe, and they stayed there for almost nine years. "Travel no longer has any charms for me," he wrote to a friend. "I have seen all the foreign countries I want to see except heaven and hell, and I have only a vague curiosity as concerns one of those." But with his business failures, it was just too expensive to live in Nook Farm. He also was hoping that the change of climate would help Livy, who was suffering from heart disease, and Jean, who was an **epileptic.**

Hideous times

Twain made several trips home while his family stayed in Europe. The **economic** situation in the U.S. kept getting worse. By the end of 1893, 500 banks and 16,000 businesses had failed. Twain knew that these "hideous times" would be bad for him, too. In 1894, his printing business failed. Fortunately for him, he had many admirers in high places. One of these was Henry Huttleston Rogers, the president of Standard Oil. A poor boy made good, and now an important businessman, Rogers decided to rescue Twain from poverty.

During the depression of 1893–94, 2,500,000 of the unemployed marched to Washington, D.C., to ask the government for help. Twain, who lost his business in the depression, had serious doubts about the effects of modern industry on ordinary people.

Henry Huttleston Rogers gave Twain much-needed advice about money. "You and I are a team," the grateful Twain told him. "You are the most useful man I know, and I am the most ornamental."

Following Rogers's advice, Twain went into voluntary **bankruptcy** in April, 1894. Rogers also told Twain to stop giving money to Paige's **typesetting** machine. Twain obeyed, but it was difficult for him to admit the machine would not make a profit after he had poured so much time, money, and energy into the project. Even after he declared bankruptcy, Twain owed people money. He was $100,000 in debt and almost 60 years old, and his future looked bleak. In Paris, on their 25th wedding anniversary, he gave Livy with a shiny silver coin. This, he seemed to be saying, is all I have left.

But Twain was already making plans for earning money to pay his debts. He made a public speech promising to pay back every penny that he owed. Now he had to raise the money, and he was determined to use his talents for speaking and writing to do it.

Grief and Guilt

Twain worked his way out of debt by turning to two things that had always earned him money in the past: speaking in public, and writing a travel book. He combined the two by researching for the book while traveling to give speeches. Starting in July 1895, he spent a year giving speeches, traveling across North America to Vancouver, and then sailing to Australia, New Zealand, Ceylon, India, and South Africa. When his tour was done, he went to Guildford, England, where he settled down to write the story of his latest travels, a book called *Following the Equator*. The tour was a popular and a money-making success. It seemed like all of Twain's worries were over.

Grief strikes

Twain, Livy, and their daughter Clara arrived in Guildford on July 31, 1896. Their other two daughters, Susy and Jean, were supposed to meet them there a week later. Instead, Twain received a letter saying that there had been a delay because Susy was sick. Clara and Livy left for home on August 15, but before they could get there, on August 18, 1896, Susy died. She was just 24 years old. Twain never fully recovered from her death. "I eat—because you wish it," he wrote to Livy. "I go on living—because you wish it; I play **billiards,** and billiards, and billiards, till I am ready to drop —to keep from going mad with grief and with resentful

Susy Clemens, Mark Twain's oldest daughter, lived from 1872 to 1896. She died suddenly while he was traveling, and her death made him feel guilty.

thinkings." Livy also had a hard time coping with the tragedy. Her heart disease made her weak, and Twain worried that she would become sicker because of the shock of Susy's death. Twain felt guilt as well as grief. He told the rest of the family that he had been selfish and neglected Susy when she was alive. "It is an odious world, a horrible world," he complained to people. But, as Livy reported, there was no question of him resting and trying to recover from Susy's death. "[He] is going on with his work," she wrote from the house they were renting in London, "but he has found it very uphill work ... He goes to his study directly after breakfast and works until seven in the evening."

While Twain was finishing *Following the Equator,* newspapers reported that he was close to death. In fact, it was a cousin, James Clemens, who was seriously ill. A reporter came to Twain's home with orders to write a 500-word article if Twain was sick, but 1,000 words if he was dead. Twain could not help seeing the comic side to this. "The report of my death," he declared, "has been grossly exaggerated!" The remark was reprinted all over the world, much to the relief of his many fans.

Following the Equator appeared in mid–1897. It had a darker tone than some of Twain's earlier nonfiction work. Also, there was more social criticism in this book than there had been in his earlier writing.

However, the book received good reviews, quickly sold 30,000 copies, and went on to become one of Twain's greatest successes. Meanwhile, on Rogers's advice, Twain had made some good **investments.** These raised more money, which helped him to pay back his enormous debts. Early in 1898 he had earned enough that he was able to pay all of his **creditors,** and still have $13,000 to spare. "For the first time in my life," he joked to Rogers, "I am getting more pleasure out of paying money than pulling it in."

Amazingly, Twain had not lost his appetite for investing in new inventions. He used his extra money to invest in a loom that wove photographs, a new cloth that was woven out of moss, and "Plasmon," a German health food that was made using skimmed milk.

Personal Recollections of Joan of Arc

Twain said that his "memoir" of Joan of Arc was written out of love and not for money. It told the dramatic tale of the fifteenth-century French heroine who believed God had told her to drive the English army out of France. After some great military successes, she was found guilty of witchcraft and burned at the stake. Twain had been fascinated by the story of Joan of Arc for a long time, and he did a lot of historical research for this project.  Writing the book may have helped him recover from Susy's death, since he used Susy as a model for Joan. *Personal Recollections of Joan of Arc* was not a Twain masterpiece, but people were interested in it, and it sold well.

The dark side of the moon

"Everyone is a moon and has his dark side which he never shows to anybody," Twain wrote in *Following the Equator*. He wrote down many of his own dark thoughts and feelings in his notebooks in the years after Susy's death. He also wrote down his bad dreams, often at great length, and started a number of projects that never came close to publication. Livy, Clara, and Jean said that he was often depressed and that he frequently lost his temper during this time.

From London, he moved the family to Vienna, Austria, where they lived in expensive hotels and were treated with enormous respect. Twain signed himself in at one of these hotels as "S.L. Clemens, Profession: Mark Twain." Twain was visited by rich and important people who had enjoyed his books, and who were entertained with his stories and jokes. Meanwhile, back in the U.S., his books were being published in an expensive 22-volume edition. He had become even more famous while he was away. "You have **pervaded** your century almost more than any other man of letters, if not quite more," wrote his friend William Dean Howells, "and it is astonishing how you keep spreading." Twain started to think about returning home to the U.S. But he took the family back to England for the summer of 1900, and they were there for the fourth anniversary of Susy's death. He wrote to a friend on that day that the tragedy sometimes seemed to have happened a century ago, and sometimes just the day before.

Twain rented a home near London in 1900. After living in hotels in large cities, Twain found it relaxing to have a home in the country.

The Returning Hero

An article about Mark Twain from the *Baltimore Sun* on April 22, 1910, shows he was a popular celebrity: *"It will be many a day before the people of the United States forget Mark Twain ... he has been one of our national celebrities, and perhaps the greatest of the clan, beaming, expansive, and kindly: a star at public feasts; the friend of presidents and millionaires ... welcome everywhere and always in good humor ..."*

By the time Twain came home to the U.S. in 1900, he had become a living legend. His books were well-known all over the country. He seemed to many to have lived out a typical American success story— not just by rising to fame from poverty, but by doing it all over again after he declared **bankruptcy** in 1894. When he returned to New York he was given a hero's welcome.

Mark Twain, back on Fifth Avenue in New York in the early 1900s, was more accepting of attention from fans and newspapers.

Twain, dressed in his trademark white suit, enjoyed playing billiards with his biographer, Albert Bigelow Paine. Sometimes he made up his own rules as he went along, to avoid hitting his cats, who slept on the table.

An opinion on everything

Twain sold his house at Nook Farm and made a fresh start with his family in New York. He also bought a house on the outskirts of Florence, Italy, where he lived with Livy from 1903 until 1904. He hoped that Livy would get better in the warm climate there. Wherever Twain went, fans and reporters dogged his every step. This kind of thing had annoyed him in the past, but now he seemed to enjoy the attention. During the time he lived in New York City, on Sunday mornings he would walk up Fifth Avenue to 59th Street and rest in the lobby of the Plaza Hotel until church was out. Then he would return home, smiling at the countless strangers on their way home from church, who lifted their hats to him or said hello.

"It always puzzled me," his daughter Clara said later, "how Mark Twain could manage to have an opinion on every incident, accident, invention, or disease in the world." He spoke often, at luncheons, dinners, and other public appearances, and his speeches were highly

47

praised. "I hate to see him eating so many dinners," commented William Dean Howells, "and writing so few books." But even as he approached 70, Twain had enough energy to write as well as to shine in public. He did appear to shine from 1906 on. That was when he decided to wear only white clothing, no matter what season it was. He declared himself to be "absolutely the only cleanly-clothed human being in all **Christendom** north of the Tropics."

Hitting out

Twain was less humorous and more critical in his final writings. He criticized religions like **Christian Science,** and public figures like the Christian Science church leader, Mary Baker Eddy. His writings criticized the "American disease" of lusting after money, and the empire-building of countries like Britain and Belgium. Also, he became a bitter opponent of the brutal business of war. Some of his darkest thoughts on modern life appeared in the collection *The Man That Corrupted Hadleyburg and Other Stories and Essays,* which he published in 1900. His criticism of modern life continued in *What is Man?,* published in 1906, and *The Mysterious Stranger,* published **posthumously** in 1916.

Twain was worried about what was happening in the world, but his personal worries at home also contributed to the less humorous and more critical tone in his writing. The house the family had rented in Florence, Italy, was full of doctors coming and going. Both Livy and Jean were in poor health. Livy was suffering from heart disease, which left her weak and nervous. Her doctor, believing that Twain's fussing over her disturbed her even more, severely limited the amount of time they could be together. Twain was desperate for Livy to get well again. When the doctor told him that Livy needed to rest, he went around attaching notes to the trees outside Livy's windows, telling the birds to keep quiet. On June 5, 1904, Livy died, after requesting Twain to play the piano and sing to her. "In my life there have been 68 Junes," Twain wrote in his notebook, "but how vague and colorless 67 of them are, contrasted with the deep blackness of this one."

Life after Livy

Twain lived for six years after losing Livy. He returned to the U.S. and built Stormfield, a beautiful mansion in Redding, Connecticut. It cost him $45,000 to build, and it was his first permanent home in seventeen years. He knew he had to keep busy to recover from his deep depression because of Livy's death. Twain played the piano, and he had always enjoyed good music. He bought a "player organ" for Stormfield, and enjoyed pumping the pedals to hear the machine play "music as played by the world's finest musicians." Twain also hired a young woman, Isabel Lyon, to serve as his secretary, housekeeper, and card partner. He called her "Lioness," and she called him "the King." Clara and Jean did not like Lyon. Twain constantly defended Lyon when they criticized her, and soon both of his daughters were avoiding Twain because of their constant arguments. In 1909, Twain's daughters discovered they were right not to trust Lyon when she was found guilty of stealing large amounts of money from Twain. Twain, Jean, and Clara made up as soon as Lyon was fired, and Clara's wedding, in October 1909, was the happiest event the family had since Livy's death. It seemed like Twain was finally getting over his depression. But soon after Clara's wedding, and just before Christmas, in 1909, Jean drowned after she had an **epileptic** seizure while she was taking a bath.

This photo of Livy and Twain was taken in New York, not long before her death. When she died, Twain was heartbroken. He wrote: "I was richer than any other person in the world, and now I am that pauper without peer."

49

Twain enjoyed playing cards. Here he is shown playing cards on his porch at Stormfield in the summer of 1908, with two of Paine's daughters and a neighbor.

Twain looks back

When Jean died, a friend wrote that Twain "was not violent or broken down with grief. He had come to that place where, whatever the shock or the turn of ill-fortune, he could accept it." The friend who noticed this was Albert Bigelow Paine. He was a children's book author, but since 1906 he had been working on a completely different kind of project, Mark Twain's *Autobiography*.

Twain enjoyed **dictating** his life story to Paine. He had so much fun telling Paine about the highs and lows of his life that the *Autobiography* has a lot of the humor that had been missing from Twain's writing since Livy died. Just like always, he mixed a lot of exaggerations with the truth. "When I was younger I could remember anything whether it happened or not," he said to Paine. "But I am getting old, and soon I shall remember only the latter."

As Twain worked on this, his last book, he was dying. He had angina pectoris, a smoker's disease that doctors sometimes called "tobacco heart." He became weaker in late 1909, when the American Plasmon Company, in which Twain had **invested** $50,000, went out of business. The end was now close. In 1835, Twain had been born with **Halley's Comet** blazing through the night sky. As the comet became visible again early in 1910, he announced, "It will be the greatest disappointment of my life if I don't go out with Halley's Comet." On April 21, 1910, Mark Twain died, with Halley's Comet overhead.

Although his sickness left him weak at the end of his life, Twain was always working, even in bed. In this photograph he is shown reading in his bedroom at Stormfield, where he died on April 21, 1910.

Mark Twain: The Man and His Work

Mark Twain once said: "All you need in this life is ignorance and confidence. Then success is sure." Few people were as successful as he was, but few wanted success as much, both as a businessman and as a writer. Although Twain was never successful in business, his failures

Twain did some of his best writing at Quarry Farm, his summer home near Elmira, New York. "To be busy," he wrote, "is man's only happiness."

in business seemed to push him to write better and better books. Like many successful writers, he often doubted his own ability. Twain regularly needed the encouragement of his family and friends to believe in himself, even as a world-famous author.

God's fool

Twain wrote some of the funniest books we have in the English language. His sense of humor made his lectures successful, too. But Twain knew that "laughter without a tinge of philosophy is but a sneeze of humor. Genuine humor is **replete** with wisdom." Twain rarely used humor just for the sake of a good joke. Many things in the world angered and depressed him, and he wanted his readers to know that the world was full of humor, but it was also full of injustice. In his lectures and **novels** he tried to educate as well as entertain. He did not always succeed in mixing humor and social criticism. Toward the end of his life, his serious side sometimes covered up the sense of fun in his books. But by then Twain had made himself a much-loved American success story.

Mark Twain was a legend in his own lifetime. He has been called "a hero of the American experience" for his journey from poverty to wealth and fame, through **bankruptcy,** and back to wealth and popularity. But, Twain described himself as a "freak," like **Halley's Comet.** He was modest about his talent for writing, and often described himself as a fool. "Ah, well, I am a great and sublime fool," he told Albert Bigelow Paine at the end of his life. "But then I am God's fool, and all His work must be contemplated with respect."

> " "[Humankind] in its poverty, has unquestionably one really effective weapon—laughter. Power, money, persuasion, persecution ... push it a little, weaken it a little, century by century; but only laughter can blow it to rags and atoms at a blast. Against the assault of laughter nothing can stand." In The Mysterious Stranger, Twain left an explanation of why he used humor to comment on society.

The Influence of Mark Twain

Novelist, travel writer, humorist, essayist, speaker, social critic, wit—Mark Twain was all of these. Although he had little education, much of what he wrote and said showed wisdom. He gained that wisdom from careful observation, hard work, and experiencing life as an "ordinary Joe," or an "Everyman," as Twain called himself.

"After writing for fifteen years," he once quipped, "it struck me I had no talent for writing. I couldn't give it up. By that time I was already famous." Twain continued to be famous long after his death. As time went by, Twain's reputation as a classic author continued to grow. Albert Bigelow Paine's book *Mark Twain: A Biography* was published in 1912. It was the first book to talk about how important Twain's writing was.

This American stamp from 1972 has a picture of Tom Sawyer on it. For many people, Twain's characters became powerful American icons—they represented the way people wanted life in the U.S. to be.

> "Mr. Clemens's books were the [record] of his life. And that life was the kind of life that the average American man of his time has believed in and admired ... He was the man that rose from the ranks without envy or **condescension** ... His genius was full of bravery, and brightness, and the joy of life."

This article in the *New York American*, on April 22, 1910, explained why Mark Twain was such a popular writer and celebrity.

> " In *Adventures of Huckleberry Finn*, Huck expresses Twain's own feelings about his talent: *"I went right along, not fixing up any particular plan, but just trusting to Providence to put the right words in my mouth when the time came; for I'd noticed that Providence always did put the right words in my mouth if I left it alone."*

A very modern man

When Twain started writing, few books were written about the lives of ordinary, everyday American people. In his travel books and in his fictional work Mark Twain gave a voice to people like these. He proved that ordinary people had interesting lives, and he was the first novelist to use the way that those ordinary people spoke to tell their stories. In doing this, he showed later authors that everyday American life was a rich and satisfying subject. Twain also created a mixture of humor and social criticism that would show up in the work of later writers. Before Twain, people thought that important books had to be serious, and humorous books were silly and forgettable. Twain proved that a funny book could also make important points about the world.

Twain was the first worldwide celebrity—someone who was well-known for being well-known. By the 1870s he was receiving enormous piles of fan mail, some of it addressed simply to "Mark Twain, The World," from his fans, who were called "Twainiacs."

Celebrities are very common now, but Twain was unusually well-known and popular for his time. Like modern celebrities, he used his fame to try to help good causes. Even as an old man he devoted time to helping Jewish victims of persecution in Russia; to the Tuskegee Foundation, a training school for African Americans, and to its president, Booker T. Washington. Twain enjoyed being recognized as a great writer, but he did not always welcome the newspaper articles about him, or the attention and letters that he got from strangers.

Twain is still receiving attention and praise from readers today. It was only Sam Clemens who died in 1910. Mark Twain lives on through his writing, especially his novels, which continues to educate readers and introduce them to his humor today.

Timeline

1835   Mark Twain is born Samuel Langhorne Clemens in Florida, Missouri, on November 30.
The Clemens family moves to Hannibal, Missouri.

1847   Twain's father dies.
Twain begins work as printer's apprentice while still at school; he probably leaves school some time in the next year.

1852   Twain publishes "The Dandy Frightening the Squatter" in the Boston *Carpet Bag*.
Twain writes occasionally for brother Orion's local newspapers.

1853–56   Twain leaves Hannibal to work as printer in St. Louis, New York, Philadelphia, Keokuk (Iowa), and Cincinnati.
Twain writes occasional pieces for journals.

1857   Twain becomes a steamboat pilot on Mississippi River until 1861.

1858   Twain's brother Henry dies.

1861   The Civil War begins.
Twain serves briefly in the Marion Rangers, a volunteer **Confederate militia,** before traveling to Nevada with his brother Orion.

1862–65   Twain works as reporter in the West, and writes comic features in Nevada and San Francisco newspapers.
He first uses the **pseudonym** Mark Twain, and publishes "Jim Smiley and His Jumping Frog."

1863   President Abraham Lincoln issues the **Emancipation** Proclamation.

1865   The Civil War ends. President Lincoln is assassinated.

1866   Twain travels to the Sandwich Islands (Hawaii) and writes about his trip. When he gets back, he has his first public speaking event in San Francisco.

1867   Twain works as a public lecturer, and travels to New York seeking wider fame. *The Celebrated Jumping Frog of Calaveras County and Other **Sketches*** is published.

1869   Twain travels to Europe and the Holy Land as a correspondent.
The Innocents Abroad is published.
Ulysses S. Grant becomes U.S. president.

1870   Twain marries Olivia Langdon in February.
Twain's son Langdon is born **prematurely.**
Twain works on the Buffalo *Express,* of which his father-in-law has given him part ownership.

1871   Twain moves to Hartford, Connecticut.
Twain's daughter Susan (Susy) is born.
Roughing It, a book about Twain's experiences in Nevada and California, is published.

1872   Twain's son Langdon dies.
Ulysses S. Grant is elected U.S. president again.

1873   *The Gilded Age,* co-written with Charles Dudley Warner, is published.

1874   Twain's daughter Clara is born.
Twain moves to Nook Farm, 351 Farmington Avenue, in Hartford, Connecticut.

1875   Twain publishes "Old Times on the Mississippi," a series of seven articles in the *Atlantic Monthly.*

1876   *The Adventures of Tom Sawyer* is published, and Twain sets to work at once on a **sequel**, *Adventures of Huckleberry Finn*.

1878–79   Twain and his family travel extensively in Europe, mainly in Italy, France, Germany, and England.

1880   Twain's daughter Jean is born.
A Tramp Abroad, a book about the family's most recent travels, is published.
Twain makes his first investment in James W. Paige's **typesetting** machine.

1881   Twain revisits the Mississippi River to research a new book. *The Prince and the Pauper* is published.

1883   *Life on the Mississippi* is published.

1884   A financial crisis in the U.S. causes many people, including Mark Twain and Ulysses S. Grant, to lose money.

1884–85   Twain organizes a lecture tour with novelist George Washington Cable.

1885   Twain turns 50 years old.
Adventures of Huckleberry Finn is published in February, and banned at the Concord Library in Massachusetts.
Twain starts his own publishing company to publish a two-volume *Personal Memoirs of U.S. Grant*.

1889   *A Connecticut Yankee in King Arthur's Court* is published.

1891   The Twain family lives in Europe—mainly England and Austria—for the next nine years.

1892   *The American Claimant* is published.

1894   *The Tragedy of Pudd'nhead Wilson* is published.
Twain goes into voluntary **bankruptcy,** mainly due to failed investment in Paige typesetter, and is rescued by Henry Huttleston Rogers.

1895   Twain begins a world lecture tour in an attempt to raise enough money to pay his **creditors.**

1896   Twain's daughter Susy dies.
Personal Recollections of Joan of Arc is published.
Mistaken reports about Twain's own death circulate in England.

1897   *Following the Equator*, the account of his lecture tour begun in 1895, is published.

1898   Twain pays off all his creditors and retains additional funds for himself and his family.
Twain's brother Orion dies.